DRY TORTUGAS
ACTIVITY BOOK

A great way to learn about Dry Tortugas National Park.
Packed with fun activities, puzzles, mazes, and more!

This activity book belongs to:

_____

Explore a 19th Century Fort and Spot Incredible Marine Life in the Crystal Clear Waters around Dry Tortugas National Park.

DRY TORTUGAS NATIONAL PARK

7
Dry Tortugas National Park is comprised of seven islands.

100
Dry Tortugas National Park covers a total area of approximately 100 square miles.

16 MILLION
Fort Jefferson, located on Garden Key, is the largest masonary structure in the Western Hemisphere with over 16 million bricks used in construction.

3RD
Dry Tortugas National Park protects significant portions of the third-largest coral reef system in the world, providing habitat for an incredible diversity of marine life.

80K
Accessible only by boat or seaplane, the park attracts 80,000 visitors annually, offering a secluded and immersive wilderness experience unlike any other.

Welcome to the enchanting world of Dry Tortugas National Park! Nestled among the turquoise waters of the Gulf of Mexico, this remote paradise is brimming with natural wonders and fascinating history. Get ready to embark on an exciting journey through this pristine marine and terrestrial ecosystem, where ancient forts stand as guardians of the past, and vibrant coral reefs teem with life beneath the waves.

IN THE MAP ABOVE:
- COLOR THE STATE YOU LIVE IN YOUR FAVORITE COLOR
- MAKE A STAR WHERE DRY TORTUGAS ISLAND IS.

HINT* IT'S OFF THE COAST OF THIS STATE:

MY PACKING CHECKLIST

- ☐ _____
- ☐ _____
- ☐ _____
- ☐ _____
- ☐ _____
- ☐ _____
- ☐ _____
- ☐ _____
- ☐ _____
- ☐ _____
- ☐ _____
- ☐ _____

SUGGESTED ITEMS TO PACK

Water Bottle!

Swimsuit + Towel

Hat, Sunglasses + Sunscreen

Comfortable Shoes/Sandals

A Lifejacket

Snacks/Energy Bars

First Aid Kit

Snorkel Gear (Mask + Fins)

Camera or Smartphone

Trail Map/Guidebook

REMEMBER TO ALWAYS PICK UP YOUR TRASH AND LEAVE THE PARK BETTER THAN YOU FOUND IT!

DRY TORTUGAS ADVENTURE BUCKET LIST

- ☐ TAKE THE SEAPLANE RIDE TO THE PARK FOR A MEMORABLE JOURNEY AND STUNNING AERIAL VIEWS.

- ☐ ATTEND ON A GUIDED TOUR OF FORT JEFFERSON

- ☐ TAKE THE SELF-GUIDED ROUTE AND EXPLORE THE HISTORIC FORT JEFFERSON AND LEARN ABOUT ITS ROLE IN AMERICAN HISTORY

- ☐ BIRDWATCH: HOW MANY RARE AND EXOTIC BIRDSPECIES DO YOU SEE?

- ☐ KAYAK THROUGH THE CRYSTAL-CLEAR WATERS AND PADDLE AROUND THE REMOTE ISLANDS OF THE PARK. (YOU CAN BRING A KAYAK ON THE FERRY)

- ☐ CAMP OVERNIGHT UNDER THE STARS ON ONE OF THE PARK'S PRISTINE BEACHES

- ☐ SNORKEL AROUND THE VIBRANT CORAL REEFS TO DISCOVER COLORFUL FISH AND OTHER MARINE LIFE.

- ☐ SNORKEL THE WRECK OF THE WINDJAMMER, AN ICONIC SHIPWRECK RESTING ON THE OCEAN FLOOR.

- ☐ ENJOY A PICNIC WITH YOUR FAMILY AMIDST THE PICTURESQUE SCENERY OF THE PARK, SURROUNDED BY NATURE.

TOP 5 FAMILY FRIENDLY HIKES

Okay, maybe they're not all exactly "hikes", but these family-friendly adventures are relatively short and easy, making them suitable for all ages. They offer opportunities to experience the diverse marine and terrestrial landscapes of Dry Tortugas National Park, and the history of Fort Jefferson, making them enjoyable and educational outings for families.

WALK THE MOAT - 0.4 MILES ~ 30 MINUTES
Enjoy a walk along the moat wall with expansive views of the ocean on one side, and fascinating views of both Fort Jefferson on the other. Keep your eye out for fish! You might spot a barracuda...

I HIKED IT AND... ☐ **I LIKED IT!** ☐ **I DIDN'T LIKE IT.**

_____

_____

BUSH KEY TRAIL - 1 MILE ~ 30 MINUTES
As long as there are no nesting brown noddies, visitors are invited to stroll the shoreline of this uninhabited island. Bush Key changes from sand to coral rubble, so footwear is recommend. Trailhead: Near Seaplane Beach

I HIKED IT AND... ☐ **I LIKED IT!** ☐ **I DIDN'T LIKE IT.**

_____

_____

FOR JEFFERSON LOOP TRAIL - 0.5 MILES ~ 30 MINUTES
Walk the upper level of the fort and follow a trail along the edges, watch out! There are no railings. A hike full of cannons, a lighthouse and incredible views.
Trailhead: Entrance of Fort Jefferson

I HIKED IT AND... ☐ **I LIKED IT!** ☐ **I DIDN'T LIKE IT.**

_____

_____

SNORKEL ADVENTURE
Discover vibrant coral reefs and marine life while snorkeling along the moat wall, or off the beach. *Suitable for families with children comfortable in the water.
Trailhead: Accessible from the beaches.

I HIKED IT AND... ☐ **I LIKED IT!** ☐ **I DIDN'T LIKE IT.**

_____

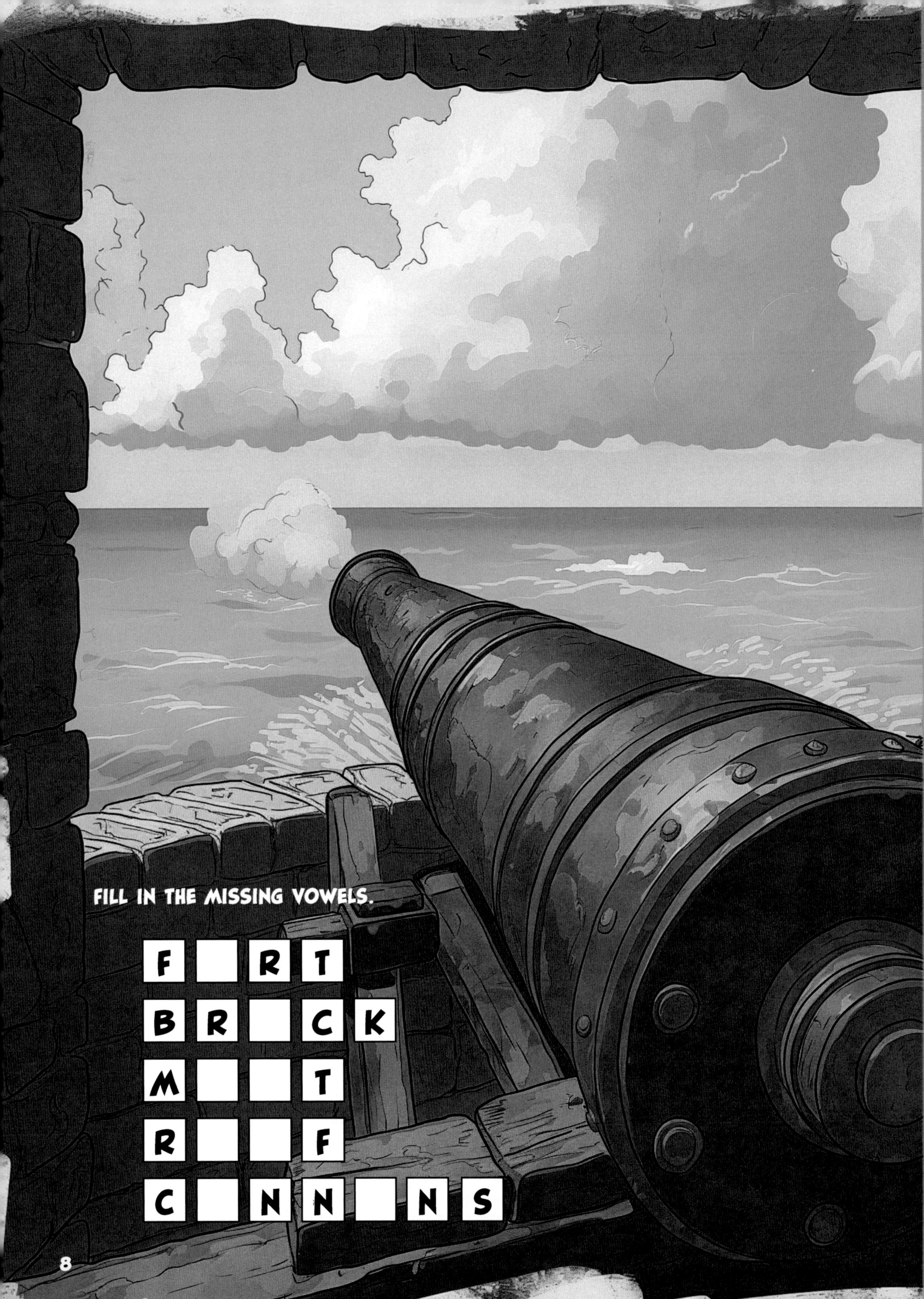

FILL IN THE MISSING VOWELS.

F ☐ R T
B R ☐ C K
M ☐ ☐ T
R ☐ ☐ F
C ☐ N N ☐ N S

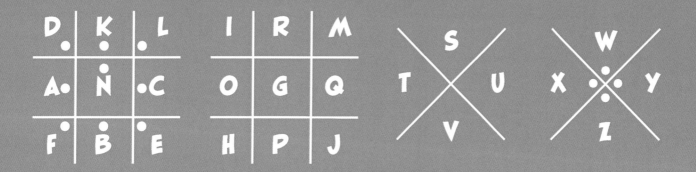

DID YOU KNOW

Named after the incredible number of sea turtles that once ruled this area, "Dry" was added after realising the island had no what?

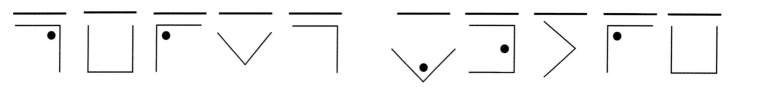

This extraordinary island is known as Dry Tortugas, home to the magnificent Fort Jefferson. Built between 1846 and 1875 using sturdy bricks, Fort Jefferson boasts an impressive array of cannons... over 450 of them! Fort Jefferson was built as a way for the U.S. Military to control the Gulf of Mexico. The 3-story fortress deterred pirates and other foreign ships from messing with U.S. trading routes.As you wander around the fort, you'll also discover a fascinating moat surrounding its perimeter, just beyond the fortress lies a breathtaking coral reef.

START

FINISH

FORT JEFFERSON IS MADE UP OF MORE THAN 16 MILLION BRICKS!

START

FINISH

FORT JEFFERSON IS ALSO THE
LARGEST
ALL-MASONRY FORT
IN THE WESTERN HEMISPHERE.

DRAW A CANNON

Follow the step-by-step instructions to learn how to draw your very own cannon!

STEP 1:
First, draw an arc line on the
left, and thin oval on the right.

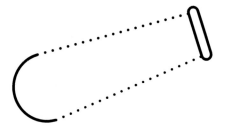

STEP 2:
Connect the top and the bottom
of the arc to the oval with 2 lines.

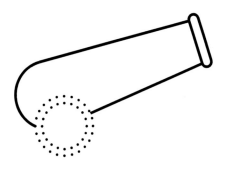

STEP 3:
Add 2 stacked circles on top of
the cannon body for a wheel.

STEP 4:
Add some straight lines for
spokes within the wheel.

STEP 5:
Add a few details, and a stack
of cannon balls.

STEP 6:
Color did it!
Now you can color it in.

A SEAPLANE ADVENTURE!

Embarked on an epic sea plane journey to Dry Tortugas National Park, where every moment is filled with wonder and adventure.

As you soar above the sparkling waters of the Gulf of Mexico, keep your eyes peeled for playful dolphins dancing in the waves below. Look down, and you might spot majestic sea turtles gracefully gliding through the sea.

As you approach Dry Tortugas National Park, get ready for the moment of awe as the breathtaking view of the historic Fort Jefferson and the emerald-green islands comes into sight.

Hold on tight as we make our descent, touching down gently on the crystal-clear waters surrounding Garden Key, a magical island paradise.

☐ **I DID IT!**
I RODE IN AN SEAPLANE!!

I FELT _____

I SAW _____

MY FAVORITE PART WAS WHEN:

_____

_____

Draw something you saw out of the window of your seaplane.

If you weren't able to take a sea plane ride, draw something you would hope to see if you could.

A shark perhaps? Or maybe a shipwreck.

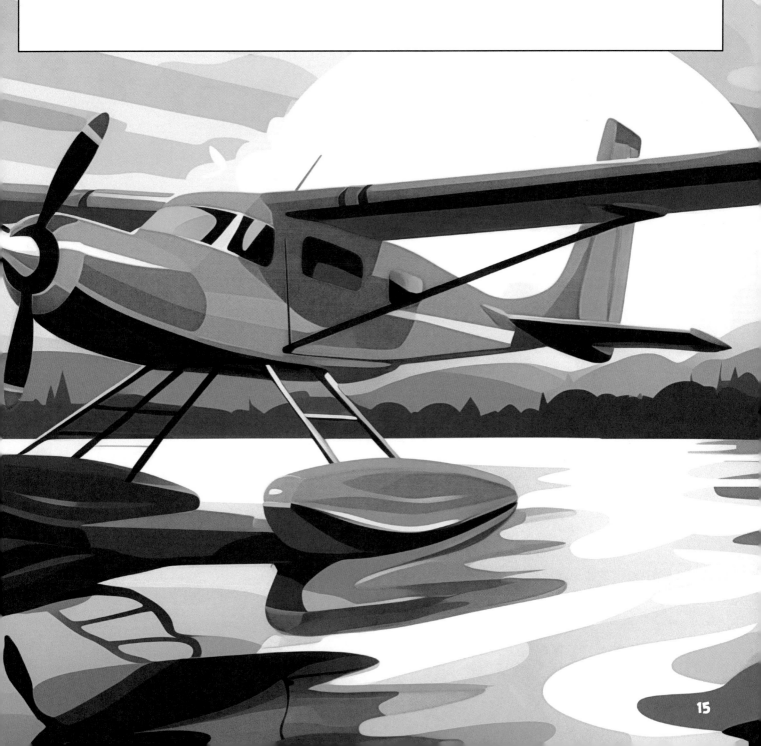

SPOT THE DIFFERENCE

Can you spot all 10 differences!?
Check off the boxes on the opposite page to keep track.

MY DAY IN THE PARK

TODAY'S DATE:

TODAY'S WEATHER:

A DRAWING OR PICTURE FROM TODAY

I BROUGHT THESE ITEMS WITH ME:

WHAT WE DID TODAY:

_____
_____
_____
_____

MY FAVORITE PART ABOUT TODAY:

_____
_____
_____
_____

RATE YOUR ADVENTURES FOR TODAY ★★★★★

MY DAY IN THE PARK

TODAY'S DATE:

TODAY'S WEATHER:

A DRAWING OR PICTURE FROM TODAY

I BROUGHT THESE ITEMS WITH ME:

WHAT WE DID TODAY:

_____
_____
_____
_____

MY FAVORITE PART ABOUT TODAY:

_____
_____
_____
_____

RATE YOUR ADVENTURES FOR TODAY ★★★★★

MY DAY IN THE PARK

TODAY'S DATE:

TODAY'S WEATHER:

A DRAWING OR PICTURE FROM TODAY

I BROUGHT THESE ITEMS WITH ME:

WHAT WE DID TODAY:

_____
_____
_____
_____

MY FAVORITE PART ABOUT TODAY:

_____
_____
_____
_____

RATE YOUR ADVENTURES FOR TODAY ★ ★ ★ ★ ★

MY DAY IN THE PARK

TODAY'S DATE:

TODAY'S WEATHER:

A DRAWING OR PICTURE FROM TODAY

I BROUGHT THESE ITEMS WITH ME:

WHAT WE DID TODAY:

_____
_____
_____
_____

MY FAVORITE PART ABOUT TODAY:

_____
_____
_____
_____

RATE YOUR ADVENTURES FOR TODAY ★★★★★

MY DAY IN THE PARK

TODAY'S DATE:

TODAY'S WEATHER:

A DRAWING OR PICTURE FROM TODAY

I BROUGHT THESE ITEMS WITH ME:

WHAT WE DID TODAY:

_____
_____
_____
_____

MY FAVORITE PART ABOUT TODAY:

_____
_____
_____
_____

RATE YOUR ADVENTURES FOR TODAY ★ ★ ★ ★ ★

MY DAY IN THE PARK

TODAY'S DATE:

TODAY'S WEATHER:

A DRAWING OR PICTURE FROM TODAY

I BROUGHT THESE ITEMS WITH ME:

WHAT WE DID TODAY:

_____
_____
_____
_____

MY FAVORITE PART ABOUT TODAY:

_____
_____
_____
_____

RATE YOUR ADVENTURES FOR TODAY ★ ★ ★ ★ ★

ANIMALS OF DRY TORTUGAS

Join us as we dive into the crystal-clear waters and explore the vibrant marine life that calls this tropical paradise home. From graceful sea turtles and speedy barracudas to colorful coral reefs and majestic brown pelicans, there's so much to discover and learn about in this fascinating ecosystem.

NURSE SHARK

Meet the Nurse Shark, a cool and calm creature of the ocean! These sharks might not be the biggest or fastest swimmers, but they sure know how to blend in with their surroundings. With their sandy-brown color and smooth skin, nurse sharks love to snooze on the ocean floor during the day. Reminiscent of a giant catsih, these sharks are super gentle and prefer to swim away from humans rather than cause any trouble.

BARRACUDA

The Barracuda fish, a sleek and speedy swimmer of the sea! With its long, silver body and sharp teeth. These clever fish are excellent hunters, using their lightning-fast speed to zoom through the water and catch their prey. Despite their fearsome appearance, barracudas are generally shy and prefer to keep their distance from humans. So if you ever spot one while snorkeling or diving, just give it a friendly wave!

BROWN NODDY

The Brown Noddy has chocolate-brown feathers and white cap, and is easy to spot as it soars gracefully through the air. These friendly birds are skilled fishermen, diving into the ocean to catch small fish and squid to munch on. On Bush Key, one of the islands in Dry Tortugas National Park, brown noddies are expert nest builders, creating cozy homes out of sticks and grass on the rocky cliffs. Please keep your distance during nesting season!

CORAL

Dive into the colorful world of coral, where tiny animals called polyps create massive underwater cities! These amazing creatures build intricate structures out of calcium carbonate, forming coral reefs that are like bustling metropolises of the sea. Coral reefs provide homes and hiding places for all sorts of marine animals, from fish and crabs to sea turtles and sharks. But coral is also delicate and needs our help to stay healthy so let's all do our part to protect these incredible underwater ecosystems!

LOGGERHEAD SEA TURTLE

These magnificent creatures are known for their large heads and powerful flippers, which help them glide gracefully through the water. Loggerheads love to munch on delicious sea creatures like crabs and jellyfish, using their strong jaws to crunch through shells and slurp up their meals. Did you know that these amazing turtles, after traveling thousands of miles all around the ocean, have such a keen sense of direction they they can find their way back to the same beach where they were born to lay their own eggs!

BROWN PELICAN

A coastal bird with a big appetite and an even bigger wingspan! These magnificent birds are expert fishermen, using their impressive diving skills to plunge into the water and scoop up fish in their stretchy pouches. Despite their size, these birds are surprisingly light on their feet and can often be seen hopping around on the beach in search of tasty treats.

KEEP YOUR EYES PEELED!
YOU NEVER KNOW WHAT CREATURES YOU MIGHT DISCOVER!

THE ANIMAL I HOPE TO SEE THE MOST IS:

ONCE UPON A TIME...

...there were millions of green turtles swimming around in the Caribbean. Sadly, today it's in the tens of thousands. That's why it's super important to protect these amazing creatures!

DID YOU KNOW?
Sea turtles can hold their breath
for up to five hours!
Talk about impressive lung power!

All five types (Loggerhead, Kemp's Ridley, Hawksbill, Green and Leatherback) of sea turtles that call Dry Tortugas home are on the Endangered Species list, which means they need extra love and care from us humans.

FILL IN THE MISSING VOWELS.

G R ☐ ☐ N

L ☐ G G ☐ R H ☐ ☐ D

K ☐ M P S ☐ R ☐ D L ☐ ☐

H ☐ W K S B ☐ L L

L ☐ ☐ T H ☐ R B ☐ C K

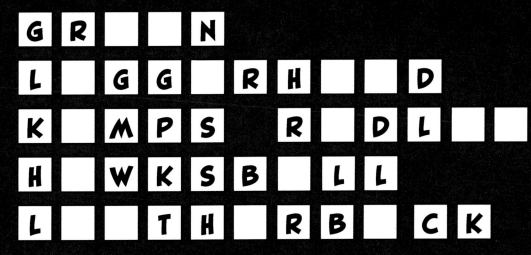

1 OUT OF 1,000

Only one out of a thousand turtles will grow up to be an adult. It's important to never touch or disturb sea turtles, and if you're lucky enough to see them nesting on the beach, keep your distance and let them do their thing in peace. If you see someone bothering a turtle and/or it's nest, please speak up to a park ranger.

TURTLE TALLY
Mark off how many
turtles you see!

STEP 1:
Draw an almond shape, for the sea turtle's shell.

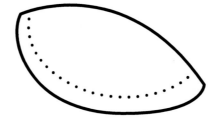

STEP 2:
Add a line slightly in from the bottom of your shell.

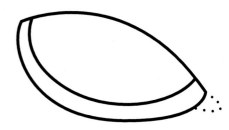

STEP 3:
Add a tail

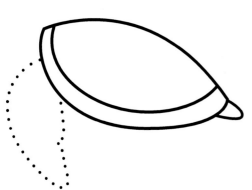

STEP 4:
Next let's add a wing shaped front flipper.

STEP 5:
And a slightly smaller back flipper.

STEP 6:
Now we can add his head. Take your time with this one!

STEP 7:
Add an eye, and if you want to, draw some shapes on his shell and limbs.

STEP 8:
Color him in!

28

DRAW A SEA TURTLE

Follow the step-by-step instructions on the opposite page to learn how to draw your very own cute sea turtle. Feel free to make any creative improvements you wish. Use the space below to practice. Happy drawing!

ANIMALS OF DRY TORTUGAS CROSSWORD

Solve the crossword puzzle by answering the questions or filling in the blanks to the clues below. All the answers can be found in this book. Use the word bank if you get stuck!

ACROSS

2 - Coastal bird with brown plumage and a stretchy pouch

5 - Slow-moving bottom-dwelling shark with a broad snout

6 - Seabird with chocolate-brown feathers and a white cap

DOWN

1 - Underwater structure built by tiny animals called polyps

3 - Sea turtle known for its powerful flippers and large head

4 - Fast-swimming fish with a sleek body and sharp teeth

CODE BREAKER

Use the key below to break the code.
Write down each letter on the lines below to uncover the answer.

D | K | L   I | R | M   S   W
A | N | C   O | G | Q   T   U   X   Y
F | B | E   H | P | J   V   Z

HOW MUCH OF DRY TORTUGAS NATIONAL PARK IS UNDERWATER?

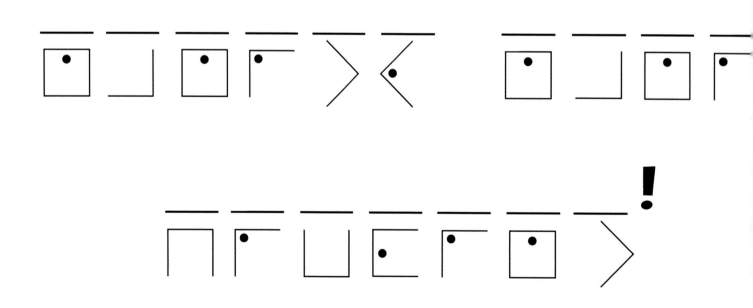

CORAL OF DRY TORTUGAS

Find and circle the names of the 6 different species of coral that can be found around Dry Tortugas National Park.

Look for the words vertically, horizontally, and diagonally.

```
U  R  R  A  A  F  K  C  T  S  T  G
S  L  O  A  S  L  N  S  L  A  H  S
R  S  U  U  L  U  I  N  R  A  P  O
T  A  G  L  U  E  A  R  C  R  R  H
R  A  H  A  L  L  L  N  S  L  H  K
S  S  C  F  N  H  R  K  R  A  L  K
O  U  A  G  S  T  A  G  H  O  R  N
L  R  C  C  P  E  S  F  F  O  R  H
N  S  T  R  N  S  F  K  U  F  R  A
N  N  U  S  R  P  I  L  L  A  R  N
A  H  S  S  O  N  L  N  A  N  I  R
S  T  A  R  S  N  L  E  A  T  G  C
```

ELKHORN	STAGHORN	PILLAR
STAR	ROUGH CACTUS	FAN

33

MY ANIMAL SIGHTINGS!

DRAW THE ANIMAL YOU SAW HERE

WHAT I SAW: _____
_____

WHERE I SAW IT: _____
_____

HOW CLOSE IT WAS: _____
_____

HOW I FELT: _____
_____
_____

DRAW THE ANIMAL YOU SAW HERE

WHAT I SAW: _____
_____

WHERE I SAW IT: _____
_____

HOW CLOSE IT WAS: _____
_____

HOW I FELT: _____
_____
_____

MY ANIMAL SIGHTINGS!

DRAW THE ANIMAL YOU SAW HERE

WHAT I SAW: _____
_____

WHERE I SAW IT: _____
_____

HOW CLOSE IT WAS: _____
_____

HOW I FELT: _____
_____
_____

DRAW THE ANIMAL YOU SAW HERE

WHAT I SAW: _____
_____

WHERE I SAW IT: _____
_____

HOW CLOSE IT WAS: _____
_____

HOW I FELT: _____
_____
_____

START

END

THE PARK IS HOME
TO ABOUT
30 SPECIES OF CORAL.

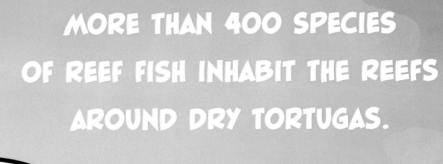

MORE THAN 400 SPECIES
OF REEF FISH INHABIT THE REEFS
AROUND DRY TORTUGAS.

START

END

START

END

LISTEN, LISTEN, WHAT'S THAT SOUND...?

Let's take a moment to sit comfortably, close our eyes, and breathe in the salty,
ocean-filled air, imagine yourself on the pristine shores,
surrounded by the soothing symphony of nature.

As you breathe in and out,
listen closely to the gentle whispers swirling around you:
the rhythmic lapping of waves against the shore,
the harmonious cries of birds,
the distant echoes of dolphins playing in the azure waters...

Feel the sunlight caressing your skin,
casting a golden hue over the ancient fortress and the vibrant coral reefs beneath

Now, in the tranquility of this enchanting sanctuary,
sketch or write about the natural sounds enveloping your senses.

WITH MY EARS, I CAN HEAR:

_____

_____

_____

_____

_____

_____

WITH MY EYES CLOSED, I CAN IMAGINE SEEING:

DRY TORTUGAS NATIONAL PARK CROSSWORD + WORD SEARCH

Use the words in the word bank to solve the puzzles.

```
S  N  E  C  P  E  N  H  O  E  U  N
L  B  L  R  E  L  A  C  S  R  I  L
R  B  E  R  L  M  R  R  F  O  C  T
L  A  N  A  I  L  G  H  L  O  L  U
T  L  N  U  C  E  O  S  O  F  R  R
R  C  R  G  A  H  T  A  T  E  L  T
S  N  P  R  N  S  N  O  R  K  E  L
N  M  T  A  A  O  E  A  L  T  A  E
S  L  O  E  A  M  O  A  T  R  S  S
N  T  L  I  G  H  T  H  O  U  S  E
P  A  C  E  O  T  R  C  L  R  S  C
R  L  O  L  R  N  L  E  A  T  G  C
```

L I G H T H O U S E

WORDBANK

Turtles   Beach

Coral   Lighthouse

Fort   Snorkel

Pelican   Moat

DRAW YOURSELF AS A PARK RANGER

AND DESIGN YOUR OWN RANGER BADGE!

MY ADVENTURES

Draw a few of your favorite memories from your adventures in the park.

DRY TORTUGAS NATIONAL PARK STAMP CANCELLATION

Immerse yourself in the beauty of Dry Tortugas National Park and create enduring memories as you embark on a journey to collect special stamps strategically placed at designated locations within the park. Inspired by the spirit of pioneers, you can engage in your own treasure hunt, each stamp serving as a tangible token of your unique adventure and a cherished memento of your time spent in this natural wonderland.

Participating in The Stamp Discovery Program is an opportunity to craft a personal keepsake. By visiting specific locations and obtaining stamps in your booklet, you are creating a visual narrative that encapsulates the essence of your experience in Dry Tortugas National Park.

Use the following page to gather as many stamps as you can from the list below. Enjoy your journey!

STAMP LOCATIONS IN EVERGLADES NATIONAL PARK:
☐ Dry Tortugas HQ – Front Desk
☐ Florida Keys Eco Discovery Center
☐ Garden Key Visitor Center

Happy stamp collecting and exploring in Dry Tortugas National Park!

MY DRY TORTUGAS NATIONAL PARK STAMP COLLECTION

DID YOU KNOW THAT THERE ARE 63 NATIONAL PARKS IN THE UNITED STATES!

HOW MANY HAVE YOU VISITED?

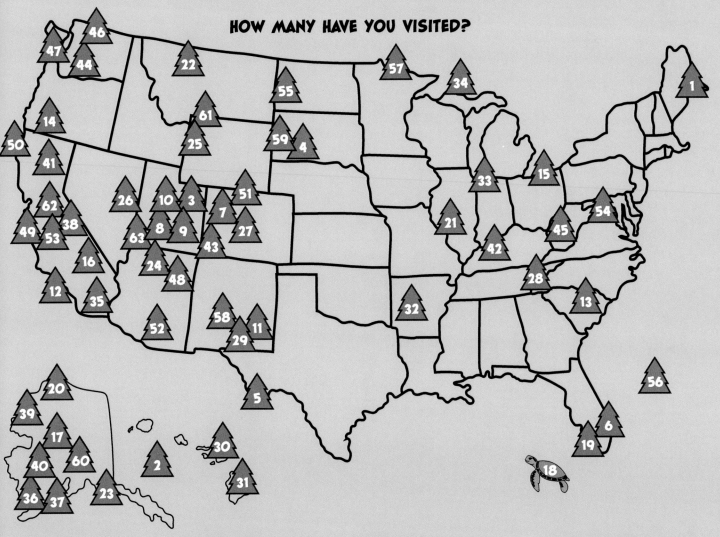

☐ 1. Acadia (ME)

☐ 2. American Samoa

☐ 3. Arches (UT)

☐ 4. Badlands (SD)

☐ 5. Big Bend (TX)

☐ 6. Biscayne (FL)

☐ 7. Black Canyon (CO)

☐ 8. Bryce Canyon (UT)

☐ 9. Canyonlands (UT)

☐ 10. Capitol Reef (UT)

☐ 11. Carlsbad Caverns (NM)

☐ 12. Channel Islands (CA)

☐ 13. Congaree (SC)

☐ 14. Crater Lake (OR)

☐ 15. Cuyahoga (OH)

☐ 16. Death Valley (CA)

☐ 17. Denali (AK)

☐ 18. Dry Tortugas (FL)

☐ 19. Everglades (FL)

☐ 20. Gates Of The Arctic (AK)

☐ 21. Gateway Arch (MO)

☐ 22. Glacier (MT)

☐ 23. Glacier Bay (AK)

☐ 24. Grand Canyon (AZ)

☐ 25. Grand Teton (WY)

☐ 26. Great Basin (NV)

☐ 27. Great Sand Dunes (CO)

☐ 28. Great Smoky Mtns (TN)

☐ 29. Guadalupe Mtns (TX)

☐ 30. Haleakala (HI)

☐ 31. Hawaii Volcanoes (HI)

☐ 32. Hot Springs (AR)

☐ 33. Indiana Dunes (IN)

☐ 34. Isle Royale (MI)

☐ 35. Joshua Tree (CA)

☐ 36. Katmai (AK)

☐ 37. Kenai Fjords (AK)

☐ 38. Kings Canyon (CA)

☐ 39. Kobuk Valley (AK)

☐ 40. Lake Clark (AK)

☐ 41. Lassen Volcanic (CA)

☐ 42. Mammoth Cave (KY)

☐ 43. Mesa Verde (CO)

☐ 44. Mount Rainier (WA)

☐ 45. New River Gorge (WV)

☐ 46. North Cascades (WA)

☐ 47. Olympic (WA)

☐ 48. Petrified Forest (AZ)

☐ 49. Pinnacles (CA)

☐ 50. Redwood (CA)

☐ 51. Rocky Mountain (CO)

☐ 52. Saguaro (AZ)

☐ 53. Sequoia (CA)

☐ 54. Shenandoah (VA)

☐ 55. Theodore Roosevelt (ND)

☐ 56. Virgin Islands

☐ 57. Voyageurs (MN)

☐ 58. White Sands (NM)

☐ 59. Wind Cave (SD)

☐ 60. Wrangell – St. Elias (AK)

☐ 61. Yellowstone (WY)

☐ 62. Yosemite (CA)

☐ 63. Zion (UT)

TOTAL: _____

BEFORE YOU GO,
THERE'S ONE MORE THING WE WANT TO REMIND YOU OF:

LEAVE NO TRACE!

It's a set of rules to help you enjoy the outdoors while also protecting it for future generations. Here are the seven principles of Leave No Trace:

PLAN AHEAD AND PREPARE.

TRAVEL AND CAMP ON DURABLE SURFACES.

DISPOSE OF WASTE PROPERLY.

LEAVE WHAT YOU FIND.

MINIMIZE CAMPFIRE IMPACT.

RESPECT WILDLIFE.

BE CONSIDERATE OF OTHER VISITORS.

ALSO: DO NOT STAND ON THE CORAL.

Remember, we want to leave the park better than we found it! Here are a few simple things you can do to help out:
- pick up any trash you see
- stay on the trail or designated swimming areas
- leave rocks, and plants where they are

Let's all work together to protect our parks and conserve the earth's natural beauty!

ANSWER KEY

PAGE 4

Locate the park on a map

PAGE 8

Missing Vowels

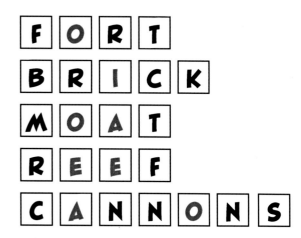

F O R T
B R I C K
M O A T
R E E F
C A N N O N S

PAGE 9

Code Breaker

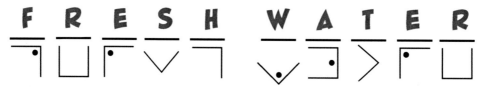

F R E S H   W A T E R

PAGE 10+11

Mazes

ANSWER KEY

PAGE 16+17

Spot the Difference

PAGE 30

Animals of Dry Tortuga Crossword

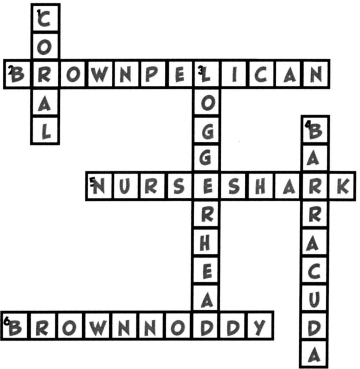

PAGE 27

Turtle Species missing Vowels

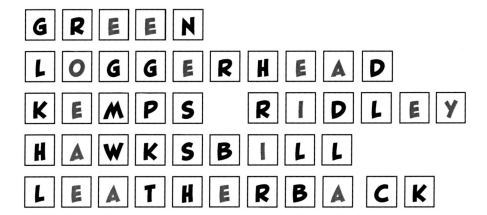

GREEN

LOGGERHEAD

KEMPS RIDLEY

HAWKSBILL

LEATHERBACK

ANSWER KEY

PAGE 32

Code breaker

NINETY-NINE

PERCENT!

PAGE 33

Types of Coral Wordsearch

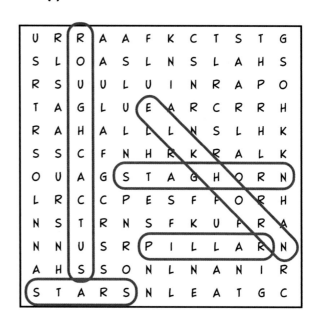

PAGE 36 + 37

Mazes

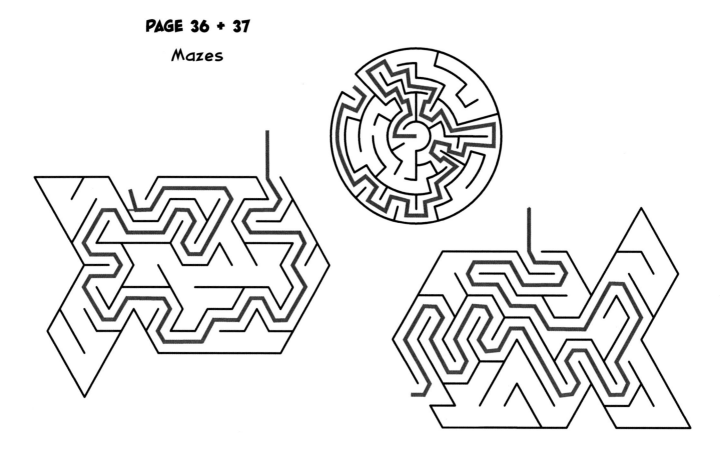

ANSWER KEY

PAGE 40-41
Wordsearch + Crossword

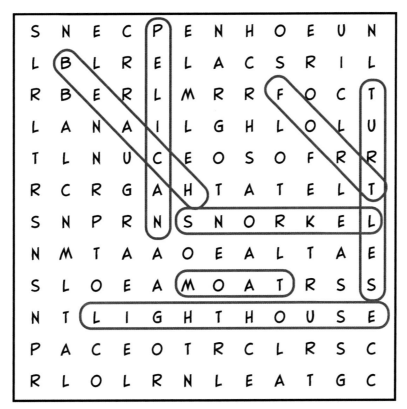

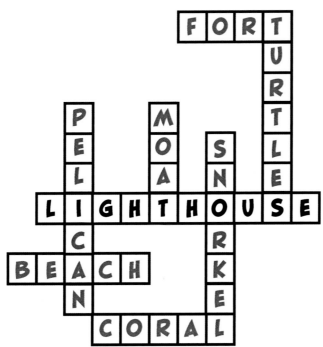

LEAVE US A REVIEW!

A Special Thank you to my children E + D for their adventurous spirits and inspiration. And also for being my product testers. :)

And to the National Park Service for all their knowledge and on-going work to protect our natural world.

CHECK OUT SOME OF OUR OTHER BOOKS!

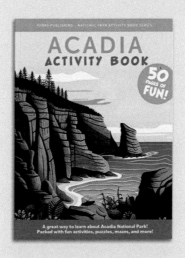

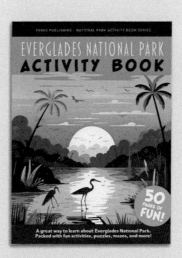

Follow Us on Instagram
@PARKSPUBLISHING to stay up-to-date with new Activity book launches!

Parks Publishing is committed to creating engaging and informative activity books for kids like you to enjoy while exploring the great outdoors. We believe that learning about nature is a vital part of understanding and appreciating the world around us.

We look forward to seeing you on your next outdoor adventure!

www.parkspublishing.com

Made in the USA
Monee, IL
03 December 2024

72321645R00036